Table of Contents

Reaching For Celestial Heights

**Uplifting, Encouraging, and
Success Poems including some
Written for Mom and Dad**

EDDIE JOHNSON

Rare Jewels Publishing Company

Copyright/Information

This book may not be reproduced in any manner without written authorization by its author. Brief excerpts in quotation marks are allowed for reviews and articles without permission. Any resemblances to individuals or incidents in real life are purely coincidental. Situational dialogue and character interactions are products of the author's imagination.

PREFACE

Reaching for Celestial Heights is a labor of love. I was inspired by my wife Hattie V. Johnson to put together a compilation of poems that would be different than the status quo; so I set out to devise such a book that would touch on a variety of topics.

This is a book of poetry written with everyone in mind. A kind word is capable of making or breaking someone's day. It's also a book where you can feast on life and religious themed poetry. The poems are perfect to recite during special occasions or engagements. At your leisure, read through each chapter of poems delighting in them. This book would make a great gift for daily hope and encouragement.

Chapter 1 - Poems of Love

"The living word provides a blueprint to the implementation of love. When it is incorporated into our daily lives it acts as a stabilizing force to keep us humble and willing to help others." - Eddie Johnson author/poet

Above The Clouds

So many tears I have shed,
Oh from the many burdens I have bared.
All my hope was gone
And yes I was all alone.
There was no coming back from my deep despair.

Then I held my head up,
And rose above the clouds

So many sleepless nights,
All from life struggles of endless fights.
I just needed someone to help lighten my load
And that would cause me to look for higher heights.
Someone that could make me forget my every care.

Then I held my head up
And rose above the clouds

I found a new love that was within me
And now I have a desire to do more.
I found a new love that was within me

Eddie Johnson

**And now I have a reason to soar
Above the clouds and to never look down any more**

The Power in Love

The power in love can heal wounded souls.
The power in love can motivate.
It can intervene in someone's hopeless state,
It has the potential for the better to influence fate.
The power in love can bind two in love.
The power in love is ever so sweet.
Making you want to tell everyone you meet,
That someone has swept you off your feet.

The power in love is eternal in the world.
It is what brings people together.
It is limited only by hate and bigotry,
However strength in love breeds unity.
The power in love is a gift to us from God.
The power in love is a lesson He has taught.
He came to earth and showed us in His earthly walk,
How we should always treat one another.
Remember God is love and there is power in love.

Eddie Johnson

Love

Love starts from within.
It then causes you to reach out.
Love is caring not just for oneself.
Love is when you can share where you have been,
Helping someone along a familiar path that they now
begin

Love is providing comfort.
Sometime we need someone to understand.
It is being there for someone who's in need.
Love is planting the fruits of your labor like a seed.
Love inspires someone to achieve their greatest
dreams.

Love's Burning Desire

A burning desire fueled by passion,
An inner glow that radiates,
Like colors brimming spring and paisley.

Love's Burning Desire

A burning desire great and sassy,
Like a jazz trumpeter tune, mellow yet sweet,
It bellows to rise.

Love's Burning Desire

A burning desire that transforms life,
Treasures unlocked shimmering.
Teams of stallions walk proudly in step

Love's Burning Desire

A burning desire is a sea that overwhelms,
With thunderous ovations seething
Grains of straws share a resemblance of wheat.

Love's Burning Desire

A burning desire a fabric of cashmere
Frolicking amongst the moon beams,
It whittles through time and memories.

Eddie Johnson

Love's Burning Desire
Love's Burning Desire

Eternal Love

Eternal Love
It's like a fire burning,
The glare from it is bright.
The feeling it brings is so right.

Eternal Love
It's like wheels turning,
On a locomotive churning,
As it moves along it's humming.

Eternal love
It's like a breeze blowing,
A never tiring desire of sharing,
Touching others with deep caring

Eternal Love
Involves warmth and closeness
Whether in good times or in sickness
Eternal love even after someone is laid to rest

Eternal love

Eddie Johnson

Do You Know What Love Is?

Do you know what love is?
It's different all the time.
Just look around and you will see,
It's not the same for you or me.
My lover may be weak for flowers,
Yours maybe for love in distant towers,
Or for someone just to talk away the hours

Do you know what love is?
It's a funny feeling deep inside
And something you cannot hide.
It radiates from within your innermost soul,
Being grateful every night for the person you hold.
Whether this person is young or old,
You know no one else will ever be able to fit their
mold

Do you know what love is?
Being able to place someone else first,
When he is sick you can be his nurse
And perhaps even his doctor.
That someone you can exchange vows with at the
altar,
Forsaken all others until death do you part,
Knowing no one else can gain your heart.

Do you know what love is?

Reaching For Celestial Heights

It brings meaning to life,
And it is capable of wiping away strife.
It's a breath of fresh air on a warm and sticky night,
Knowing that you have met Mr. or Mrs. Right,
And that you will never tire of their sight.

Do you know what love is?
It's caring and wanting to be closer in spirit and
truth.
It's a journey in a letter meant for you and your
honey.
When it's cloudy with you it's sunny
I'll always find your jokes funny.
Knock - knock on the door.
I am yours for evermore.

Do you know what love is?
It's a smile that is only for you.
It's a special chuckle that is shared by two.
Souls that are bonded by glue
Someone that you love to greet each day anew
Someone worth more than all the riches in the world,
Knowing he will always be your man and you his girl

Do you know what love is?
It's different all the time,
Just look around and you will see,
It's not the same for you or me

9

Eddie Johnson

Love Is Meant To Stand The Test Of Time

Love is meant to stand the test of time.
Though lovely - it's not all about flowers,
Nor being whisked away to stay in foreign towers.
It can be found in words you say
You should tell your mate you love them every day.

Love is meant to stand the test of time.
A warm feeling within your innermost soul,
That can be felt by the person you graciously hold.
Whether that person is young or old,
You should love them even more than you love
yourself

Love is meant to stand the test of time.
Comforting them as if you are a nurse,
Providing care and cures to their ills when they hurt.
Yes, you are a doctor of love.
Remember to provide them the attention they
deserve.

Love is meant to stand the test of time.
It is what gives meaning to life.
When your partner pains it can wipe away strife.
Never take their needs for granted.

Reaching For Celestial Heights

They should feel safe and secure whenever you are
near.

Love is meant to stand the test of time.
It's caring and wanting to be closer each day.
You don't have to knock on the door to their heart,
You already have the key to it.
Something about you makes them feel ten feet tall.

Love is meant to stand the test of time.
A smile that only you can bring
It's about souls that are bonded by glue.
Someone you look forward to being with,
Love is something that the world's riches can never
buy.

Love is meant to stand the test of time.
Simply put it never changes - it's the same everyday.

Eddie Johnson

Loving

Loving is such a sweet feeling.
Loving is a connection not only to oneself.
Loving is being on a wavelength with everyone else.
It's reaching out to others by fellowshipping.
It's making a difference in the world through caring.
Seeing others that are in need and not turning your
head.
Extending a hand to help them out instead,
Let them know you are there for them.

"Sometimes we may aspire to go farther in our lives, embarking on new frontiers. These new undertakings could present challenges that with the help of God could be less of a struggle." - Eddie Johnson   author/poet

Reaching For Celestial Heights

**Not just scaling the mountain to reach its peak,
Or soaring thru space to eventually come in for a
landing,
There is a power that defies all logic and
understanding.**

**Just remember God is always in control
When you are: Reaching For Celestial Heights**

**The present may be bleak but the future could be
bright.
Don't take the easy way out when there is work to be
done.
Look to the one who made the earth, the moon, and
the sun.**

**Just remember God is always in control
When you are: Reaching For Celestial Heights**

Follow the golden rule blue print to eternal life

Eddie Johnson

Sometimes pressures of the world will cause you to
frown.
Don't go around walking with your head hanging
down.

Just remember God is always in control
When you are: Reaching For Celestial Heights

Knowing You Have Arrived

You know you have arrived
When you are cognizant of where you have been.
When you can look around and see your fruits,
That came from all your efforts and pursuits.

You know you have arrived
When you are cognizant of things known and unseen
When you have positioned yourself to enjoy life,
In the face of present and future strife

You know you have arrived
When you are cognizant of people that surround you
When you can gain attention for being an asset,
From those you know and haven't met.

If you can truly say these things,
Then you know you have arrived.

Eddie Johnson

Sure

Without a doubt,
Finding the way out,
Even when no one else will even try,
Your desire is to reach for the sky.

If you are striving for success,
You need to be SURE.

Never wavering,
You're focusing in,
Keeping your eyes on the prize,
Eventually it will materialize.

If you are striving for success,
You need to be SURE.

You know what you want,
Every step of the way,
Ready to meet your challengers,
Paying no attention to hecklers

If you are striving for success,
You need to be SURE.
You need to be SURE.

Faith

'

Faith is believing beyond the comprehension of
another
Seeing promise in something that is going nowhere

Faith is to know in advance your efforts will be
rewarded

Faith is to paint a picture in life you derived from a
thought
Faith is to know the end results from battles to be
fought

Faith goes the extra mile to chase down the elusive
dream

Faith is not letting oneself be put in the proverbial
box
Faith is to know you can break through the glass
ceiling

Faith is to know you will be victorious after battling
giants.

Faith can take you to the next level in life

Eddie Johnson

Successful

To achieve a desired result
And receive gratification from a fight well fought.
To prevail after conquering your enemy,
And you now can live to see tomorrow.
If you can beat the odds against you -
You are successful.

To see a goal in life come to fruition,
It's to be good at something whether it's a hobby or
profession.
To help others to realize their true potential,
To build confidence in those who are despondent.
If you can beat the odds against you –
You are successful.

Jump For Joy

It happens Automatically
You jump for joy.
Like a kid with a new toy,
You jump for joy.

You did it.
It really does fit.

It happens Automatically
You jump for joy.
The results are in your favor,
You jump for joy.

Hard work paid off,
You are no longer distraught.

It happens unexpectedly
You jump for joy.
You found someone you love.
You waited your whole life
For the person that is oh so right.
You jump for joy.

It happened!

Eddie Johnson

Mission Accomplished

I tightened the last screw
Then I observed the finished product.
It was a work of art.
He was just a tiny tot as he watched dad at work.
The track was now laid.
The locomotive was positioned
And the cars attached.
I flipped the switch and it came to life.
Departing the station it was on its way.
It twisted and turned throughout the town and
hillside.
He chuckled and laughed and I was elated.

Mission Accomplished.

Gathering Steam

Moving along the path laid out in the plan,
Details were checked to complete the task at hand.
Needed support staff was added to help you to move
forward,
While all along you were Gathering Steam.

Full Speed Ahead,
Don't look back for too long,
Only looking back to know where you come from.

Full Speed Ahead,
Keep your eyes on the prize,
Speak of your progress it will help you to rise.

Moving along the path laid out in the plan,
You can now see the finish line in the sand.
Everyone's spirits lifted and they began to cheer,
While all along you were Gathering Steam.

You have finally arrived,
It's time to reap your reward.
Everyone enjoyed their part although the journey was
hard,
While all along you were Gathering Steam.

Eddie Johnson

Bask

Wallow in your accomplishment,
Delight in it as a result of ultimate fulfillment,
You defied the odds and you quieted the naysayers.
You have received the answer to your prayers,
You are brimming over with confidence due to your
success.

Holler out a scream of jubilation,
Embrace and congratulate those that helped you.
It was great that they stuck with you to see you
through.
For this you now have for them an unending
admiration.
You are standing on top of the mountain you have
conquered

To this end it's only right that you should BASK!

The Proof Is In the Pudding

So you want to know how it was done,
Well the proof is in the pudding.

And how might that be?
Please do tell me.

As you can tell it has the right mix,
The right ingredients make the recipe.
Go ahead give it try.
I've tried it myself and I know it will fly.

Umm it's not bad,
It's the best I've had.

Were going to make a killing on this
And as you can tell the proof is in the pudding.

Eddie Johnson

Success

You have reached the terminus of joy and
satisfaction.
Wrought from hard work you now have gratification,
Borne from your stated implications,
Rewarded for your supplications,
Not giving into temptation
And you now have final compensation for your
success.

You have now reached the pinnacle of final
measurement.
From this you will rejoice in its pure merriment,
From time that was well spent,
Culminating in your ascent,
After watching every cent
You now have acknowledgement for your success.

The Time Has Come

The time has come for celebration.
You stuck it out for the long run,
You are now standing on top of the world.
Your dream has now become a reality
And it's available for everyone to see.

The time has come for celebration.
The cause for your new sensation,
It's a very unique and awesome revelation.
Go out and celebrate throughout the town.
You're on a high and may never come down.

Eddie Johnson

Rolling In The Dough

You are now at the top of your game.
You are in position to get what you want.
They know for your game to show,
For you the extra mile they must go
And you're going to be rolling in the Dough

It's time to throw caution to the wind,
Go out paint the town from end to end.

"In the process of doing the Lord's will we should pray to garner strength to overcome obstacles that are thrown in our paths." - Eddie Johnson   author/poet

The Office Water Cooler

Standing by the Office Water Cooler,
Listening to the daily chatter,
I was getting to know the different rungs on the
ladder.

Standing by the Office Water Cooler,
Reminiscing about worldly affairs,
Watching coworkers ruffle and split hairs,
I was getting to know the different rungs on the
ladder.

Standing by the Office Water Cooler,
Trying to find myself among the players,
Never listening to the naysayers,
Plotting and charting myself towards the top,
I was getting to know the different rungs on the
ladder.

Eddie Johnson

Jet

Waiting for departure,
I prayed that all would go well.
I had acquired knowledge to excel.
I checked to make sure that I was secure in my seat.

I began to taxi.
Closing my eyes briefly,
I felt the plane lift off the ground.
I began to be acclimated to my new work place.

Turbulence set in,
When I started feeling safe,
The plane rocked from side to side.
I was a fighter capable of taking on job related strife.

Soon the dark sky cleared,
My ride again became smooth
And I wondered why I even feared.
My hard work confirmed I was a problem solver.

The journey continued on,
The crew performed like all stars,
They served their passengers with great respect.
I became one of the company's great supervisors

I enjoyed the experience,
Although the journey it was long.

Reaching For Celestial Heights

The ride seemed to have ended too quickly.
But I felt all and all the time was well spent.

The flight neared its destination.
The plane started in its descent.
I closed my eyes briefly.
The landing gear came down.
The landing was soft.
My career ended.

Eddie Johnson

Office Politics

Someone once said to me,
You'll be just fine on your new job,
That is if you want to be,
Then you'll have to avoid the office politics.

You need to avoid gossip,
Avoid invading other people's space,
And don't be overly hip,
Don't allow yourself to succumb to the office politics.

Be considerate of the opposite sex,
Don't be accused of providing unwanted advances,
That could cause you to become an ex,
So don't become a part of the office politics.

Don't become the office bully,
At work people don't need added pressure.
Just try to do your job fully
And you'll be just fine if you avoid the office politics.

Office Cheerleader

The Office Cheerleader,
Knows employees birthdays,
She also keeps track of the kitty.
She gets cards and sweets for the money.

The Office Cheerleader,
She heads the office parties,
And selects the places where they are held.
She also makes sure that everyone is invited.

The Office Cheerleader
She keeps track of happenings
From Funerals, weddings and fundraisers
She is the one that informs everybody of all things.

Eddie Johnson

Work

Well I'm told it's only work if you don't enjoy it.
If you like what you are doing it just time well spent.
You get up each day looking forward to another day
of fun.
It's like an unending day at the beach of pure
relaxation,
Your chores are like events that you do for recreation.
There is nothing to shun.
Only things you want to get done.

Well I'm told it's only work if you don't enjoy it.
No one can deter you from your myriad of task on
hand.
What you do is like a good product that you know by
brand,
You just consume it each day again and again.
It doesn't matter that it is the same.
To like what you do
Makes you want to greet each day anew.

"Sweet is the journey that we partake, which will lead us to our heavenly destination. Our testimonies of his goodness as we go along our way should draw others to our Lord and Savior." - Eddie Johnson author/poet

Oh My Jesus, He's The One To Fix It

When you feel try'n to hold on to your many dreams
That you're down hearted,
Oh my Jesus, He's the one to fix it.
Yes learn to lean and depend on Him.

With Him you can solve problems that you have to day,
Just to Him learn to pray
And I'm sure He will make you feel better.

Remember He's the way the truth and the life
And that's why I say,
Oh my Jesus, He's the one to fix it
Yes learn to lean and depend on Him.

With the Lord right at your side to help and guide you,
Yes you can make it through
And He'll make all your life so much brighter.

Eddie Johnson

He can make the blind to see, deaf to hear
And the lame to walk,
Oh my Jesus, He's the one to fix it
Yes learn to lean and depend on Him.

With the Lord no problems are too large or small,
He'll see you through them all,
Just open up your heart and let Him in
Oh my Jesus, He's the one to fix it.

That's Why I Praise Thee Lord

Whenever I need Him, He's by my side.
Whatever in life I desire, I know He can provide.

That's Why I Praise Thee Lord.

He helps me to be strong each day,
Helping me along life's treacherous way

That's Why I Praise Thee Lord.

Thank you Lord, thank you for keeping me strong.
Thank you Lord, thank you for helping me when
things go wrong

I praise you Lord.
I praise you Lord.

I will forever praise Thee Lord.
I will forever praise Thee Lord.

Whenever man knocks me down,
He dusts me off - he lifts me from the ground

That's Why I Praise Thee Lord.

Everything in this world belongs to him,
Not to you, I or them.

Eddie Johnson

That's Why I Praise Thee Lord.

Thank you Lord, thank you for keeping me strong.
Thank you Lord, thank you for helping me when
things go wrong

I praise you Lord.
I praise you Lord.

I will forever praise Thee Lord.
I will forever praise Thee Lord.

You are worthy of all my praise,
In my life story you have been on every page.

That's Why I Praise Thee Lord.

You are worthy my God,
Yes - You are worthy my God.

A Witness

A Witness for my Lord:
Means to share my belief,
Live a Christian life and to be a fisher of men.

A Witness for my Lord:
Means to extend my hand,
I should tell others about the Lord's heavenly promise
land.

A Witness for my Lord:
Means to be someone that cares,
I should feed the hungry with physical and spiritual
food.

Eddie Johnson

My Journey Home

Lord I wouldn't take nothing for My Journey Home.
I came to you in desperation when I was all alone,
You reached out and comforted me in your
lovingness,
And Lord one day I know I'll go home with you to
rest.

Lord I wouldn't take nothing for My Journey Home.
I'm a witness for you Lord - I'm in your discipleship,
I revel in bringing the lost to you, Lord.
Oh Lord I just thank you for all you do.

Lord I wouldn't take nothing,
Lord I wouldn't take nothing for My Journey Home.

Joy

Joy, Sweet Joy cometh in the morning,
I know my work down here is done
And I might not see the morning sun.
But I'm looking up toward heaven
I've received my invitation to be welcomed in.

Joy, Sweet Joy cometh in the morning,
I can feel a refreshing breeze,
It's coming at me putting me at ease.
Off in the distance I can see the light,
It's a heavenly light shining so bright.

Joy, Sweet Joy cometh in the morning,
I can hear the angels, they are singing,
The chariot I can see is swinging down.
Oh I know, yes Lord, I am heavenly bound,
It's been hard down here but I'm finally going home.

I'm going to find Joy, Sweet Joy in the morning.

Eddie Johnson

Be Therefore Ever So Mindful

Be therefore ever so mindful
How the light in your life had come to dim
And then you reached up to Him.
He wrapped His arms around you
And forgave you then took you in.
Remember where you came from
And how He helped you

Be thankful everyday
He has given you one more day on earth to stay.
He could have let you go by the wayside
But you found in Him, you could confide.
He heard you and answered your prayer
And you have a complete makeover.
Stay grounded in Him.

Be therefore ever so mindful
Think of the reward that awaits you.
Don't turn back, temptation will come
And it will go just tell the devil no.
You are headed for heavens shore
And when you get there you'll know.
You'll be there for ever mo.

Be therefore ever so mindful
You're going to jump and shout
And to Him give continual praise.

Reaching For Celestial Heights

Oh I can hear myself now
Saying Lord, I just want to thank you,
Thank you, Lord I just want to thank you
For being so good to me
And I will be therefore ever so mindful.

Eddie Johnson

Grace

Heavenly love is like no other.
He bared the cross all by Himself.
He showed mercy and favor for a dying world.
He gives us all a chance,
All we have to do is take the right stance.

Heavenly Father I am your child.
Lord, teach me and guide me.
I now want to walk with thee.
What must I do in order to be with you?
I want my soul to be brand new.
I went to church and heard the minister say
And because of you, He has shown GRACE.
Believe, repent and accept him as your Lord and
Savior.

Our Heavenly Father

You are my brother
And darling you are my sister.
Let's put aside our differences
And give thanks to Our Heavenly Father

Put aside our weapons,
Teach our daughters and our sons.
Let them know we are all of one family.
Praise Christ Jesus Our Heavenly Father.

God so loved us,
He gave us His only son.
In spite of all we've done.
Oh be grateful to Him Our Heavenly Father.

Eddie Johnson

A Walk With God

A walk with God is a way of life.
It's not to be taken for granted,
It should be shown in the way you speak
And even in the company that you keep.

A walk with God is oh so sweet.
He has made my life complete,
Just follow the golden rules of love
To one day be with Him above.

Still Standing

They said I was done and that I did not stand a
chance.
But through the grace of God I'm still here.
He healed my body and took away my every fear
And for Him I am grateful.

I'm Still Standing.

The Lord took my hand and I became under His
guidance.
I drew closer in my walk with the Lord.
Now I share His blessings and how He came aboard.
He righted my ship.

I'm Still Standing.

He still came through despite my wrongdoings and
faults.
He knew for me how to provide the right results.
That's why I don't mind being a living testament.
My God is eternal.

I'm Still Standing.
I'm Still Standing for Him.

Eddie Johnson

Ingredients Of Love

Sitting on my front porch swing back in the woods of
Georgia,
The night was blacker than black
As I think back
I decided I needed a lift because I had fallen down so
far.
I wanted to get up,
So I jotted down what I felt was the Ingredients of
Love.
I looked to the best teacher I could;
That's my Lord and Savior sitting above.

He taught me about sweetness like from the
honeysuckle tree
That should be within me
Like a sweet bee.
How a juicy steak flavor can be enhanced with just
the right spice
I think how I must live a Christian life.
I think of how Christ loved us so much that He died
for our sin.
He is the ultimate lover of men.
He has the kind of love I need within.

He taught me about how we should break bread
together.
How we should always help one another

Reaching For Celestial Heights

Like Christ Our Father.
We should never think it is too much of a bother,
To give someone in need a piece of bread
Or a place to lay their head
He is the cooling water that we should have within
So we never thirst again.

"Life is given to us through the heavenly bread we are fed and heavenly water we drink." - Eddie Johnson author/poet

A Rich Life

A billionaire felt alone,
Falling to his knees he cried out to the Lord,
You have provided me with everything I asked
But yet Lord I feel poor.
If I gave it all back maybe I could be happy.
He looked up toward Heaven and said teach me
Lord, show me how to be truly rich.
He reached over grasped the Holy Bible
And he learned how to care for those less fortunate.
He used that which he had been given to help others.
Now humble and considerate to his brothers and
sisters,
He learned to tell others about the glory of God.
He let them know they should keep God's
commandments.

Years later he fell to his knees,
He said thank you Lord for teaching me
And showing me how to be truly rich

Living Is

Living is not merely surviving,
It is constantly rising.

Living is a feeling of accomplishment,
It is having fulfillment.

Living is a feeling of being complete within,
It is enjoying something again and again.

Living is to have time to spend away from problems,
While surrounding yourself with love ones.

Living is not worrying about money.
It's having more days that are sunny.

Eddie Johnson

My Life

My life
I started out slow
Then I took my first step
And then things began to flow.

I surrounded myself with friends.
They were near when I needed help.

I found myself always on the go
And I wanted to know more and more.
I knew knowledge was the key to unlock the door,
This would allow me to attain flight so that I could
soar.

Life's Stairway

I looked upwards from the first stair,
I realized there would be a long journey ahead.
I embarked on the first flight of steps,
Without a worry or care

I rested after reaching the first landing,
I noticed the stairway twisted in a new direction.
On the second floor others joined me.
We had a thirst for knowledge.

Life's unexpected complications began to occur.
I spent a lot of time on the second landing.
I wondered if I should go any further,
Everything was such a bother.

Eventually I journeyed to the third floor,
I found others and we had a time of sharing.
I really enjoyed our brief time together,
They helped me to feel better

From the third landing I looked up again,
The stairway twisted and turned in a new direction.
Some of my friends got off on the fourth floor,
We waived goodbye.

On the fourth landing I felt rejuvenated,
I and others continued on to higher heights.

Eddie Johnson

I finally found someone I really cared about,
A real soul mate

On the fifth floor we connected intellectually.
After the next landing the stairway twisted again.
My mate's creativity was about to take her away from me,
She would follow her dreams.

I left my mate behind on the sixth floor,
We kissed and she took the awaiting elevator.
I immersed myself completely in work and study,
I was now into self gratification.

On the seventh floor I spent time reminiscing,
I wished my lover would return to make me complete.
I started seriously looking for love once more.
My attempt to find love was unsuccessful.

I spent a short time on the next landing before continuing.
The awaiting floor door opened and she returned.
We continued to climb Life's Stairway.
Life was good now.

"We should always have a place to go for earthly solace; in heaven we will have everlasting peace." - Eddie Johnson author/poet

Home Is

Home is a place to go at the end of the day
And the pressures of the world should go away

Home is a place where you can truly be yourself,
Try to unwind, and think of nothing else.

Home is a place to be shared by family.
There they should live together in harmony.

Home is a place to go when I leave this earth,
To reside in heaven upon rebirth

"A strong mother has traits including those that are spiritual, which will help her family to shine." - Eddie Johnson author/poet

That's My Mom

When I was young,
She was there to wipe away my tears,
She was there to calm all my fears.

Full of love,
That's my mom.

And as I grew,
She was there with good advice.
She would steer me from all vice.

Full of love,
That's my mom.

Now I am grown,
She still helps me to stay strong,
No matter what in life may go wrong.

Full of love,
That's my mom.

A Real Mother

A mother's love is untiring.
She realizes the first nine months was just the
beginning.

A mother's love is unwavering.
She understands that she could never turn her back
on her child.

A mother's love is unique.
She has a strong relationship to her offspring and it is
never weak.

A real mother
A real mother's love

A mother's love is nurturing.
She helps to mold, shape and guide her child with
loving hands.

A mother's love is caring.
She hurts when her child does and rejoices when the
child succeeds.

A real mother
A real mother's love

Eddie Johnson

She Was Always There

Every since I can recall she was always there,
Reaching out, picking me up, and dusting me off
when I fall.

Teaching me, fervently directing me,
She always reminded me of the importance of
education.
She said knowledge can open windows and doors in
the world.

She Was Always There
Always There

Every step of the way she was always there,
She helped me with problems to navigate perceived
obstacles.

She was an example of a real life role model.
The way she carried herself inspired me to be strong.
When you looked at her, you knew she was the real
deal.

She Was Always There
Always There

Every time I looked around she was always there.

Reaching For Celestial Heights

She emphasized the importance of treating everybody
fair.

She believed everyone should find a way to help
others.
She used her talents and abilities to facilitate change.
She taught me I should want to do the same.

She Was Always There
Always There

Every phase of my life she was always there,
She was there in sickness and good health for better
or worse.

She knew that strength always came from within.
She said do the right things and you'll be the better
for doing so.
My life has been enhanced for having her as my
mother.

She was Always There
Always There

A good mother is always there.

Eddie Johnson

Mama

What makes a Mama?
She's a down home type lady.
She knows how to make cornbread from scratch
She knows the importance of family dinners.

What makes a Mama?
She's the glue that holds her family.
She knows everything about her offspring and
siblings.
She's the one in which all of her family members
confide.

What makes a Mama?
She's one that has humor and wit.
She thrives to keep them close knit.
She entertains her family and helps them to relax.

What makes a Mama?
Mama is always in control.

A Mother's Love

A mother's love is cuddling.
It provides warmth.
It provides the ultimate comfort.

A mother's love is unending.
It shows strength
And it's never defeatist.

A mother's love is heart warming.
It is caring,
She teaches her child about sharing.

A mother's love is consoling.
A virtuous beauty,
She shines for her child to see.

Eddie Johnson

Motherhood

Motherhood

Even if father could not usually mother could.
She was never so tough,
That she would not listen
Mother always knew her stuff

Motherhood

Hold on dad lest give them the benefit of the doubt,
Hear what they have to say.
You don't want to run them away,
That's why so many children go astray.

Motherhood

She could exude strength while imparting wisdom.
Even if you did wrong,
She knew you would need some help to hold on.
Your mother would always do her very best

"Dad should be a pillar for his family. Through his example they are shown how to weather storms. Our heavenly Father leads his flock." - Eddie Johnson   author/poet

Good Old Dad

He is known as Good Old Dad.
He stands out from all others.
He has set standards for me, my sisters, and brothers.

We thrive to measure up
We know he is watching us.
The bar has been raised and he will not settle for mediocrity

He tells us to strive to be the best we can be
And that is what he wants to see.

He is known as Good Old Dad.
He understands his children are unique.
We'll need to learn to stand on our own feet.
He supports us in our goals and aspirations.

He helps us maneuver through life phases.
He lends a hand when it is requested,
When our own efforts can be proven and tested.
We should always give our best effort.

Eddie Johnson

**Though his ways may seem hard,
Good Old Dad is just teaching us how to be strong.**

My Father's Wish

He never had much when he was growing up,
Anything they had was never enough.
He and his siblings always had to share.

My Father's Wish was that I would always have
more.
He had to struggle for every dollar
And tried to stretch the money so it could go farther

He never had a chance for education.
He worked the fields in the heat.
He still knew knowledge would be the key
To make his dream for me complete.

My Father's Wish was that I would always have
more.
So I worked hard to be a scholar,
Obtained various degrees all in his honor.

He has now passed on to the great beyond
But he told me before he left that he was satisfied.
I'm grateful he was always on my side
And that I carried out My Father's Wish.

Eddie Johnson

Dad Is The One

Dad is the one

He provides for his family.
He teaches humility,
That true strength comes from being humble.
We should never be so brazen as to cause others to stumble.

Dad is the one

He is an example for his family
He has a love for God.
He talks about our heavenly Father and his love.
God died for our sins before he ascended above.

Dad is the one

He spends time with his family.
Solidarity,
He says that we should always help one another.
We should always encourage each other for the better.

Dad is the one
Dad is the man!

My Dad

He was hard working.
He believed in being a provider for his family.
He wanted his children to succeed.
He wanted us to have opportunities he never had.
He wanted that because he was My Dad.

He was a fisherman.
He believed his wife was his greatest catch.
He enjoyed talking about his children.
He thought of us as his prized possessions.
He felt that way because he was My Dad.

He was humorous.
He enjoyed making people laugh.
He marveled when they could share together in love.
He believed in having fun because he was My Dad.

Dad is gone now
But I still love him.
I'll always remember him
And will be grateful that he was My Dad.

"I think of a wife as a mate that brings to the table companionship, which makes both spouses complete. If you have the Lord by your side then you will never be alone." - Eddie Johnson author/poet

My Wife's Love
(Written for my wife, Hattie Vanesa Johnson)

**My wife's love is like the wind.
It's a breeze that blows hope and encouragement.
She cares about the children of the world
And believe they should have a solid Christian
foundation.
She believes change for the better can be fostered in
youth.
I know this is true because she has shown that she
cares.**

**My wife's love is like a soothing melody.
Her love plays out a tune of peaceful tranquility.
Like the strings of a harp her sound is crystal clear.
She lifts her voice in songs of praise to her Lord.
Words emanating from her often reflect her
spirituality
She knows God should be a vital part of life for her
family.**

My wife's love is like a ship on the sea.

Reaching For Celestial Heights

I commend her for always being on course for our
daughter.
She is a pillar of strength, a well full of wisdom,
And a spring that sprouts forth from a fountain that
is refreshing.
She is the cooling water that is within her home.
She truly understands the meaning of being a mom.

My wife's love is like a burning flame.
She provides warmth to me in dealing with the cold.
She stands with me and realizes that there is strength
in unity

You're a wonderful woman,
I'm grateful to have you as my wife.

Eddie Johnson

A Joyous Wife

If you have A Joyous Wife,
You are blessed to have her in your life.

If you have A Joyous Wife,
She helps you over the rough roads of strife.

If you have A Joyous Wife,
She knows how to bring a smile to your face.

If you have A Joyous Wife,
She is like fruit on the vine that is always ripe.

A Precious Gift Of Love

Like a rare diamond,
My wife shines within my life.
Sparkling in every way,
Even in the words she say,
She is truly A Precious Gift of Love.

I watch her in her sleep.
I feel good lying by her side,
Knowing she has chosen me
To spend her eternity,
She is truly a Precious Gift of Love.

Like the spring time,
She has always been a fresh breeze.
Putting my mind at ease,
She always aim to please,
She is truly a Precious Gift of love.

Eddie Johnson

My Better Half

My Better Half

We are now joined in holy matrimony.
We are now one.
My world is so sweet,
Since I have met my special honey,
She makes my life complete.

My Better Half

She provides something I've always wanted.
She's a gentler side of me.
She's soothing and comforting.
She's a spirit of tranquility.
She's there whenever I need to be rejuvenated.

My Better half

She makes my life just that much more.
My days are sunnier,
My nights are warmer,
Just to have her near is worth more than silver or
gold.

"A husband should be in charge of helping his family to grow spiritually. He should look to the Lord for daily guidance as he walks in the Word of the Lord. - Eddie Johnson   author/poet

Why Does A Husband Exist?

A husband exists to make his wife happy.
He knows her every materialistic desire.
He knows what's needed to spark her fire.

He knows when he has screwed up,
That calls for her favorite flowers.
When her spirits are down,
He makes her laugh, and forget about all others.

A husband exists to make his wife happy.
He knows his role as the head of his house.
He knows the time with his wife has to be of quality.

He knows when she is angry,
That chocolate always makes her sweet.
Whenever she is tense,
He knows how to massage her feet.

A husband exists to make his wife happy.
He likes sharing adventures with her near or far,
He understands in her life he must always be a star.

Eddie Johnson

He knows when she pouts,
That he has got to let her have her way.
She is the one that can always make his day,
For that he should be grateful.

A husband exists to make his wife happy.
He enjoys showering her with expensive jewels,
They show how much he values her.

He knows he has to walk on water
And perform any other feats to protect her.
He was put in her life for a reason
And for him to be happy they must be together.

A husband exists to make his wife happy.

Mr. Fix It

I'm a husband.
I fix things when they break.
I mend them whether they are physical or emotional.
I am the head of the family,
I'm in charge of making sure that everybody is
happy.

I'm a husband.
I am the chief disciplinarian.
When Mom is unable to bring order,
It is my responsibility as the father.
I know my children delights,
I am the one to intervene in stopping fights.

I'm a husband.
I fix things when they break.
I have to stay on top of my game.
I can never take my role for granted.
If I do there is no one else to blame

Eddie Johnson

A Husband

A husband is devoted to his family.
Although there are others in his life,
There is no doubt of his number one priority.
After God his responsibility is to his children and
wife.

A husband is the head of his household.
His job is not just to show he is in control.
He understands his children sometimes need
guidance.
On issues he seeks help from God to take the proper
stance.

A husband knows how to be romantic.
He knows how to keep his wife satisfied.
He provides gifts she desires to keep her smiling wide.
Unified in their Christian belief they stand side by
side.

Strong Hands

He stood tall, so sure, and so successful.
He stood tall, able to inspire, and so resourceful.

He was my guide along life's treacherous roads,
Whether highways with quick routes to destinations
Or byways full of stops and tumultuous terrains.

He was always there when I needed strong hands.

He brought joy, mounds of pleasure to my soul.
He brought joy, brought me warmth when I was cold.

Soaring in a plane traveling throughout the heavens,
He was in the cabin reading gauges keeping my life on
course.
He provided wisdom, knowledge, and needed
protection.

He was always there when I needed strong hands.

He was a rock, capable of sustaining hard knocks.
He was a rock, someone of whom I could lean on.

He was a durable and mighty fortress from the storm,
When the rains would come and the winds would
blow.
He was someone I could go to when things got rough.

Eddie Johnson

He was always there when I needed strong hands.

He taught me, how to love and to give of myself
He taught me to help others and to do it not for fame.

I was in his classroom and he was my favorite teacher.
He followed his lesson plan and I always did my
homework.
He helped to mold me into the person I am today.
He was always there when I needed strong hands.

"Daughters in the ministry of the Lord are taught to console and to assist others in need." - Eddie Johnson   author/poet

My Daughter

She will always be my little girl.
She is a bright spot in my world.
I'll always wish the best for her,
No matter where in life she goes.
Her sparkling personality flows.

My Daughter
My Little Girl

She enjoys the company of others.
She always does what is right.
She believes that dreams do come true
She believes one should be up to the fight
No matter what in life they pursue

My Daughter
My Little Girl

Eddie Johnson

Daddy's Girl

She is a little girl that has always been rough.
She hung out with her brothers and they made her
tough.
She is not a girl that likes playing with mom's cookie
dough.

She likes doing things with her father.
She likes taking trips with him to go camping.
She treasures the time with him hiking and fishing.

She is a little girl that looks up to her father.
She emulates his work ethic to become better.
He taught her to exude strength and not to just settle.

A Good Daughter

A Good Daughter,
She likes spending times with her mother.

A Good Daughter,
Don't mind standing up to protect her little brother.

A Good Daughter,
Find ways to share common interest with her father.

A Good Daughter,
Relish having a friend that is also her sister.

A Good Daughter,
Realizes the love of her family makes her better.

"Good sons are groomed to be competitors in their daily lives and protectors of their families. The Lord is a Sheppard that watches over and cares for his flock. - Eddie Johnson author/poet

A Father's Son

A Father's Son

To Dad he is the one,
He grooms him to carry on his name.
That means he has to stay on his game.
He teaches him how to be a man.
He teaches him on his own two feet to stand

A Father's Son

To Dad he's a sport,
He roots for him on the field or on the court.
He's a point guard in basketball.
He's a quarterback in football.
In life he is the one that will make the call

A Son

A son is to be treasured.
He brings joy and loves to compete.
He is taught to be a good sport even in defeat.
His love can not be measured.

A son has to show strength
Because he knows society expects it.
He'll be called upon to be a protector
And knows he has to meet the challenge.

A son is mom's little gentle fellow.
Around the house he's dad's helper
He is always willing to help out.
He steps in when dad is on the go.

Eddie Johnson

A Mother Looks At Her Son

A mother looks at her son,
She sees a miniature version of his father.
His father teaches him to be a protector,
One day he'll have to be the king of his own castle.

He studies his father, every move he makes.
Throughout life he watches how he navigates.
He sees his father being successful at work.
At home he shows that love doesn't have to hurt.

A mother looks at her son,
She notices the good work of her husband.
He took his role seriously
And her little boy is now a man.
He has a very solid foundation on which to stand.

About The Author

Eddie Johnson is a Florida native that continues to evolve as an author and poet constantly refining his writing. At an early age he discovered this unique gift. With the urging of his spouse, he decided to share the results of his literary prowess with the world. For now and the foreseeable future he'll continue to transform life experiences into interesting storylines. Billionaire's Retreat, a romance, murder mystery, and suspense thriller is his most recent work. The focus of this African American fiction writer will be on urban romance, murder suspense, and dramatic street related topics. Throughout his life he's held jobs assisting others. For over a decade he worked as a Public Assistance Specialist with the State of Florida. Since then he has worked in private sector customer relations and billing related positions in telecommunications and banking. He has a Degree in Business Data Processing. Eddie is a devoted husband and father.